Table of Contents

You Can Do AI: How Non-Coders Can Create, Design & Automate with AI Tools

You Can Do AI: How Non-Coders Can Create, Design & Automate with AI Tools

Part I:

Understanding AI Without the Code

1. Welcome to the Age of AI

In this chapter, we'll dive into the exciting world of artificial intelligence (AI) and explore how it is transforming our daily lives—without requiring coding expertise. From voice assistants to smart recommendations, AI is already part of the fabric of modern technology. But what exactly is AI, and how is it accessible to non-programmers?

What is AI, Really?

Artificial Intelligence, or AI, refers to machines or systems designed to mimic human intelligence. At its core, AI enables computers to learn, reason, solve problems, and make decisions. You've probably encountered AI without realizing it—think of the recommendations on Netflix or the auto-corrections on your phone.

In its most advanced forms, AI can be used to generate text, create art, recognize patterns, and even assist in decision-making. However, you don't need to be a programmer to leverage AI in your work or personal life. With the rise of no-code and low-code tools, AI has become more accessible to entrepreneurs, marketers, educators, and creators of all kinds. These tools enable you to harness the power of AI without writing a single line of code.

The Rise of No-Code & Low-Code AI

The world of no-code and low-code tools has skyrocketed in popularity, offering easy-to-use platforms that allow anyone—regardless of technical background—to build and deploy AI applications. No-code tools typically rely on visual interfaces that enable users to drag and drop components, creating powerful AI-driven apps without having to write complex code. On the other hand, low-code tools offer a simplified version of coding, allowing for customization with minimal programming knowledge.

These tools are revolutionizing industries by reducing the barrier to entry for non-technical users. Entrepreneurs can now automate tasks, marketers can generate targeted ad content, and educators can create personalized learning experiences— all with the help of AI. In this book, we'll guide you through some of the most popular AI tools that require no programming knowledge, helping you unlock the potential of AI in your work.

With no-code and low-code platforms, AI becomes accessible to everyone, and the possibilities are endless. Whether you want to automate a process, generate creative content, or even build your own AI-powered app, the tools and knowledge you'll gain here will empower you to do so—without the need to write any code.

2. Why You Don't Need to Code

In this chapter, we'll debunk the myth that you need to be a skilled programmer to take advantage of AI tools. With the rise of no-code and low-code platforms, you can unlock the power of artificial intelligence without writing a single line of code. Whether you're an entrepreneur, a marketer, or a content creator, you can start using AI tools to enhance your work, automate tasks, and even create entirely new products—all without needing to be a technical expert.

Breaking the Myth of Programming Prerequisites

For years, the world of technology and artificial intelligence has been reserved for those with specialized knowledge in coding and computer science. If you wanted to develop AI-powered applications or leverage machine learning, you needed to be familiar with complex programming languages like Python or R. This barrier discouraged many from even considering the possibility of using AI in their business or creative endeavors.

However, the landscape has changed dramatically in recent years. Today, powerful AI tools have been democratized, and the need for programming skills has significantly diminished. Platforms like **ChatGPT**, **Midjourney**, and **Zapier** have made it possible for non-technical users to harness the full potential of AI, from generating text and images to automating workflows, all through simple user interfaces.

No-code and low-code platforms have bridged this gap by providing intuitive tools where you simply input your requirements and let the AI do the heavy lifting. Whether you're crafting content, automating emails, or analyzing customer data, these tools allow you to do so with minimal or no programming at all.

The myth that programming is a prerequisite for using AI is now just that—a myth. Thanks to these innovative platforms, anyone can tap into the power of AI, regardless of their technical background.

Use Cases for Non-Technical Users

While it may sound too good to be true, non-technical users can leverage AI to streamline workflows, enhance creativity, and improve productivity in ways that were once reserved for programmers or data scientists. Here are some real-world use cases for AI tools that don't require coding skills:

1. **Content Creation and Marketing:**
   o **AI Text Generation**: Platforms like **ChatGPT** enable marketers and content creators to generate blog posts, social media captions, newsletters, and more—just by providing a prompt. These tools can even be used to rephrase or rewrite content to avoid plagiarism.
   o **SEO Optimization**: Tools such as **SurferSEO** and **Writesonic** help optimize content for search engines, automatically generating keyword-rich content suggestions, improving readability, and enhancing your content's SEO value without any coding knowledge.

2. **Visual Design and Art Generation:**
   o **Image Creation**: With tools like **Midjourney** and **DALL·E**, you can generate custom images, illustrations, and even logos by simply describing what you want. Whether it's for marketing materials, social media posts, or branding assets, these platforms make it easy to create professional-grade visuals without a designer.

   o **Graphic Design**: **Canva**, which incorporates AI features, allows users to design presentations, social media posts, and promotional materials by choosing from pre-made templates and customizing them with AI-powered suggestions.

3. **Task Automation:**
   o **Workflow Automation**: **Zapier** and **Integromat** enable users to automate repetitive tasks without writing any code. For example, you can set up a "zap" that automatically posts new blog articles to social media, or sync your CRM with your email marketing software, saving hours of manual work.

- o **Data Integration**: AI tools can automatically pull data from one platform and push it to another, ensuring you never have to manually transfer information again. This is particularly useful for businesses that need to streamline data between tools like Google Sheets, Slack, or Trello.

4. **Customer Support and Service:**
    - o **Chatbots**: AI-powered chatbots (like **ManyChat** or **Tidio**) can be set up easily to respond to customer queries on websites or social media platforms. These bots can be used to guide customers, answer common questions, and even offer product recommendations—all without the need for programming.
    - o **AI Virtual Assistants**: Use tools like **Jasper AI** to automate customer service responses, schedule appointments, or manage basic administrative tasks for you. With simple triggers and workflows, your assistant can handle a wide range of tasks efficiently.

5. **Education and Training:**
    - o **Personalized Learning**: AI can help educators create personalized learning plans for students. By using platforms like **Khan Academy's AI Tutor** or **Quizlet**, teachers can assign tailored exercises and quizzes that adapt to each student's learning pace and style.
    - o **Content Creation for Courses**: Non-technical users can create entire online courses using AI-powered tools to generate lecture notes, quizzes, and assignments, all while saving significant time.

These examples show that AI isn't just for tech professionals—it's a tool that can enhance the productivity and creativity of individuals across industries. No-code and low-code platforms have leveled the playing field, allowing anyone to integrate AI into their daily workflows. So, whether you're crafting your next marketing campaign or designing the perfect customer support experience, AI tools make it easier than ever to get started—no programming required.

3. Essential AI Concepts, Simply Explained

In this chapter, we'll break down some key AI concepts that are essential to understanding how AI tools work. These concepts are not only fascinating but also incredibly useful for anyone looking to harness the power of AI without needing a technical background. Whether you're a marketer, entrepreneur, educator, or content creator, understanding the basics of AI will help you use AI tools more effectively and unlock their full potential.

Machine Learning vs. Generative AI

AI is a broad field, and within it, there are various types of algorithms and models designed to solve different kinds of problems. Two of the most popular areas of AI today are **Machine Learning (ML)** and **Generative AI**. Let's take a closer look at each:

1. **Machine Learning (ML)**:
    o   **Definition**: Machine Learning is a subset of AI where algorithms are trained on data to make predictions or decisions without being explicitly programmed for specific tasks.

- How it works: In ML, a model "learns" from examples (or data). For instance, if you're training a machine to recognize images of cats, you would feed the algorithm many pictures of cats, and the model would learn the features of a cat (like shape, size, and color). The more examples it gets, the better it becomes at predicting whether a new image contains a cat or not.
- Example use case: ML is used in tools that recommend products on e-commerce websites (like Amazon) based on your past browsing history, or for spam email filters that get better at identifying unwanted emails over time

2. **Generative AI**:
   - Definition: Generative AI refers to a type of machine learning that creates new content, such as text, images, music, or videos, based on patterns it has learned from data.
   - How it works: Rather than just making predictions, Generative AI actually generates new data that mimics what it has seen in its training data. For example, Generative AI models like **ChatGPT** generate human-like text based on the prompts they are given, while **DALL·E** can generate entirely new images based on textual descriptions.
   - Example use case: A marketer might use **ChatGPT** to generate ad copy or blog posts. An artist could use **Midjourney** to create unique artwork by describing their vision.

The key difference is that **Machine Learning** typically focuses on analyzing and predicting based on existing data, while **Generative AI** is designed to create new, original content.

Natural Language Processing (NLP)

Natural Language Processing (NLP) is a field of AI that focuses on the interaction between computers and human language. The goal of NLP is to enable computers to understand, interpret, and respond to text or voice data in a way that mimics human understanding.

1. **Definition**: NLP involves the use of algorithms to process and analyze large amounts of natural language data. This includes everything from speech recognition to machine translation, text summarization, and sentiment analysis.

2. **How it works**: NLP systems break down language into smaller components, such as words or phrases, and understand the structure, meaning, and context behind those components. For example, NLP models like **ChatGPT** are trained on vast amounts of text data to understand language patterns, meaning, and nuances. When you input a prompt, the model uses this understanding to generate a coherent, contextually relevant response.

3. **Example use case**:
   o **Chatbots**: NLP enables chatbots to understand and respond to customer inquiries. If a customer asks a question like "What are your business hours?", an NLP-powered chatbot can quickly understand the intent and give an accurate response.
   o **Sentiment Analysis**: NLP is also used to analyze customer reviews or social media posts to determine the sentiment behind them—whether they are positive, negative, or neutral. This helps businesses improve customer experience.

Image Generation and Automation

AI is not just for text—image generation and automation are also becoming increasingly popular applications of AI. These

**You Can Do AI: How Non-Coders Can Create, Design &
Automate with AI Tools**

tools allow anyone, regardless of artistic ability, to create high-quality images or automate image-related tasks with just a few inputs.

1. **Image Generation**:
   - **Definition**: Image generation using AI involves creating new images based on text prompts or pre-existing images. Generative AI models like **DALL·E** or **Midjourney** can take descriptive text inputs (e.g., "a futuristic city at sunset") and generate original artwork or photographs that match the description.
   - **How it works**: These models are trained on vast datasets of images and learn to understand the relationships between words and visual concepts. When you provide a prompt, the AI uses this training to synthesize a brand-new image that aligns with your description.
   - **Example use case**: A content creator could use Midjourney to generate unique visuals for social media posts, website banners, or even book covers, simply by describing what they want.

2. **Image Automation**:
   - **Definition**: Image automation refers to using AI to speed up tasks related to image editing, such as resizing, color correction, or background removal. AI can also be used to categorize or tag images based on their content.
   - **How it works**: AI tools can analyze the contents of an image and automatically make adjustments. For example, a tool like **Remove.bg** uses AI to automatically remove the background of an image, saving hours of manual work.
   - **Example use case**: An e-commerce store could use AI-powered image automation tools to quickly prepare product photos for their website, ensuring that all images are uniform, properly cropped, and ready for upload with minimal effort.

Understanding these core AI concepts gives you a clearer picture of how different AI tools work and how they can be applied to everyday tasks. Whether you're generating content, automating workflows, or designing images, having a grasp of Machine Learning, Generative AI, NLP, and Image Generation will help you make the most of the no-code and low-code tools at your disposal. In the next chapters, we'll dive deeper into how to use these tools in practice and unlock their potential for your personal and professional projects.

Part II:

Hands-On with Tools

Husn Ara

ChatGPT for Everyday Tasks

In this chapter, we'll explore how ChatGPT, one of the most powerful AI tools available today, can make everyday tasks easier and more efficient. Whether you're writing content, brainstorming ideas, conducting research, or managing customer interactions, ChatGPT can serve as your virtual assistant, saving you time and energy while boosting your productivity.

Writing, Brainstorming, Research

1. **Writing**:
   ChatGPT is an excellent tool for generating high-quality written content quickly and easily. Whether you're drafting blog posts, social media captions, emails, or reports, ChatGPT can help you create coherent and engaging text in minutes. You can provide a simple prompt, and ChatGPT will generate a draft that you can refine or use directly.

   - o **Example**: You need to write a blog post about the latest trends in digital marketing. Simply provide ChatGPT with a prompt like "Write a blog post about the top 5 digital marketing trends in 2025." It will create a well-structured post with ideas and suggestions.

2. **Brainstorming**:
   ChatGPT is also a fantastic brainstorming tool. If you're stuck in the creative process, whether it's for new product ideas, content topics, or strategies,

ChatGPT can offer fresh perspectives and generate a list of ideas you might not have considered.

- o **Example**: If you're a content creator looking for blog ideas, you can ask ChatGPT, "Give me 10 unique blog post ideas for a fashion website." ChatGPT will provide a list of creative suggestions that you can use as inspiration.

3. **Research**:

   ChatGPT can assist with quick research, pulling together information from various sources to help you understand a topic more clearly. While it doesn't replace in-depth research or expert opinions, it's a great starting point for gathering summaries, explanations, and insights on any subject.

   - o **Example**: If you're researching how artificial intelligence is impacting education, you can ask, "What are the main ways AI is transforming education?" ChatGPT will provide a concise, relevant answer that you can build upon.

Customer Service & Personal Assistants

1. **Customer**   **Service**:

   One of the most common uses of AI, particularly for businesses, is in customer service. ChatGPT can be used to handle customer queries, provide support, and even troubleshoot problems—all without human intervention. By using ChatGPT as a chatbot on your website or in your email system, you can offer instant, round-the-clock assistance to your customers.

   - o **Example**: A customer asks, "How do I return a product I bought?" ChatGPT can immediately respond with the return policy, steps to initiate the return, and any other relevant information, ensuring the customer has a seamless experience.

2. **Personal   Assistants**:
ChatGPT can function as your personal assistant, helping with a wide range of tasks, from scheduling meetings to sending reminders or even drafting quick responses. By integrating ChatGPT into your workflow, you can automate many aspects of your daily routine and focus on more high-level tasks.

o   **Example**: If you need to send out an email reminder about an upcoming meeting, simply prompt ChatGPT with "Write a reminder email for my meeting tomorrow at 10 AM." It will generate a professional message for you to send.

Prompt Crafting: How to Get What You Want

While ChatGPT is a powerful tool, its effectiveness depends on how clearly you communicate your needs. Prompt crafting is the art of writing specific, well-thought-out prompts to ensure that ChatGPT understands your request and generates the best possible response.

1. **Be Specific**: The more details you provide, the better the result will be. Instead of asking a broad question like, "Tell me about AI," try something more specific, like "Explain how AI is used in healthcare to improve patient outcomes."

2. **Use Follow-Up Prompts**: If you need more information or clarification, don't hesitate to ask follow-up questions. ChatGPT can build on previous responses, so feel free to ask it to expand, narrow down, or explain certain points in more detail.

o   **Example**: After asking about AI in healthcare, you could ask, "Can you give an example of a hospital using AI in patient diagnosis?"

3. **Experiment with Style and Tone**: ChatGPT can write in various styles and tones. Whether you need formal, casual, persuasive, or creative writing, you can specify your preferred tone in your prompt.

   o **Example**: "Write a casual email to a colleague asking for an update on the project," or "Write a formal letter to a client explaining a delay in service."

4. **Iterate**: If the first response isn't exactly what you want, try refining your prompt. ChatGPT is highly adaptable, and with a few adjustments, you can get the response that best suits your needs.

   o **Example**: If the generated text is too short, you can prompt, "Expand on this explanation with more examples and details."

By mastering prompt crafting, you can make ChatGPT an even more effective tool, ensuring that it delivers precisely the results you need. Remember that clarity, specificity, and experimentation are key to getting the best outcomes.

In this chapter, we've explored how ChatGPT can assist with writing, brainstorming, research, customer service, and acting as your personal assistant. With the right prompts, this powerful AI can become an indispensable tool in your daily tasks, helping you work smarter and faster, no coding required.

Husn Ara

Visual Magic with Midjourney & DALL·E

In this chapter, we will explore how you can harness the power of AI to create stunning visuals, whether you're designing marketing assets, product mockups, or even original artwork. Tools like **Midjourney** and **DALL·E** have revolutionized the creative process, allowing anyone to generate professional-grade visuals using nothing more than text prompts. Let's dive into how you can use these AI tools to bring your ideas to life.

Creating Art, Product Mockups, and Marketing Assets

1. **Creating** **Art**:
   Midjourney and DALL·E are powerful AI models capable of generating unique artwork based on descriptive prompts. Whether you're an artist or someone who needs visuals for a project, you can use these tools to create one-of-a-kind pieces of art.

   o **Example**: If you're looking to create an abstract painting, you can simply enter a prompt like "Abstract painting of a sunset over mountains with vibrant colors and geometric shapes," and the AI will generate an original piece of art that matches your description.

   o **Use case**: Artists or content creators can use AI-generated art for website designs, social media content, album covers, and more.

2. **Product** **Mockups**:
   For entrepreneurs, designers, or marketers, creating product mockups has never been easier. You can generate realistic 3D mockups or conceptual designs without needing any design skills. Just describe your product, and let the AI handle the rest.

   - **Example**: If you have a new phone case design, you could input a prompt like "Create a photorealistic mockup of a phone case with a minimalistic geometric design in muted colors." The AI will generate a highly detailed, realistic image of the product based on your description.

   - **Use case**: Businesses can use AI to generate product mockups for presentations, e-commerce sites, or promotional materials, speeding up the product development process.

3. **Marketing** **Assets**:
   Marketing teams can use Midjourney and DALL·E to create eye-catching ads, banners, social media posts, and more. The AI tools make it easy to generate professional visuals quickly, saving time and resources compared to traditional design methods.

   - **Example**: For a digital marketing campaign, you might prompt, "Design a vibrant and dynamic banner for a summer sale featuring tropical elements, bright colors, and bold typography." The AI will generate a visually appealing banner that is ready for use in your campaign.

   - **Use case**: Marketing teams can produce high-quality assets for social media, websites, email newsletters, or digital ads— all without the need for a graphic designer.

Prompt Engineering for Design

While Midjourney and DALL·E are intuitive tools, getting the best results often requires careful crafting of your prompts. **Prompt engineering** is the process of refining your prompts to ensure the AI understands your vision and generates exactly what you want.

1. **Be Detailed but Concise**: The more specific you are in your prompt, the more control you'll have over the final design. However, it's important to keep your prompt clear and concise so that the AI can generate accurate visuals without getting confused by too many details.

   o **Example**: Instead of saying, "Create a design for a website," say, "Create a clean, modern homepage layout with a large hero image, white space, and a call-to-action button below the fold." This gives the AI a clear direction for your design.

2. **Use Descriptive Language**: Use vivid language to describe the mood, style, color palette, and any other details that are important to your design. If you're aiming for a specific aesthetic or visual style, mention it in your prompt.

   o **Example**: "Generate a vintage-style logo with a retro font, warm colors like orange and teal, and a coffee cup graphic." By including these specifics, you help the AI understand exactly what you want.

3. **Experiment with Styles and Formats**: AI tools like Midjourney and DALL·E can generate images in a variety of styles, such as photo-realistic, cartoonish, abstract, or artistic. If you have a particular style in mind, be sure to mention it. You can also specify the format, whether you want a portrait, landscape, 3D render, or vector-style image.

   o **Example**: "Create a photorealistic rendering of a laptop with a minimalistic design, clean lines, and a matte finish," or "Design an abstract geometric illustration with pastel colors and soft gradients."

4. **Use Iterative Refinement**: Don't be afraid to refine your prompts as you go

along. If the first design isn't quite right, you can tweak the prompt by adding or removing details. Sometimes, even small changes in wording can lead to significantly different results.

- o **Example**: If a first attempt comes out too busy, refine your prompt to say, "Simplify the design by reducing the number of elements and focusing on a minimalist style."

5. **Leverage Variations and Enhancements**: Both Midjourney and DALL·E allow you to create variations of an image once the initial design is generated. This feature lets you explore multiple design options and refine your ideas further.

- o **Example**: After getting an initial design, you can ask for a variation of that design with a different color scheme, or perhaps with additional elements like a tagline or different background.

By mastering prompt engineering, you can harness the full creative potential of AI and produce high-quality visuals for a wide range of projects. Whether you're an entrepreneur in need of product mockups, a marketer looking for eye-catching assets, or a creator wanting to generate unique art, Midjourney and DALL·E can become indispensable tools in your creative toolkit.

In the next chapter, we'll explore how to combine these AI-generated visuals with your broader business strategies and how to integrate them into workflows for maximum impact.

Husn Ara

Automating Workflows with Zapier + AI

In this chapter, we'll explore how you can streamline your business processes and personal workflows by automating tasks using **Zapier** and AI-powered tools. Zapier allows you to connect different apps and automate repetitive tasks with no coding required. When combined with AI, it opens up new possibilities to enhance efficiency, reduce manual work, and increase productivity. Let's dive into how you can use Zapier and AI to supercharge your workflow.

Connecting Apps with No Code

1. **What is Zapier?**
   Zapier is an online automation tool that connects over 2,000 apps, such as Gmail, Slack, Google Sheets, and Salesforce, enabling them to work together without writing a single line of code. With Zapier, you create workflows called **Zaps**, which consist of a **Trigger** and one or more **Actions**.

   o **Trigger**: An event that starts the automation. For example, receiving a new email in Gmail could be the trigger.

   o **Action**: The task or action that happens automatically once the trigger occurs. For instance, if the trigger is a new Gmail email, the action could be saving that email's attachment to Google Drive.

Example use case: You can set up a Zap to automatically save all email attachments you receive in Gmail into a specific

25

folder on Google Drive, reducing the need to manually save files.

2. **Setting Up Zaps:**
The beauty of Zapier is that you don't need technical skills to set up these workflows. By simply choosing the apps you want to connect and defining the trigger and actions, you can automate almost any task in your business or personal life.

   o **Example:** Automatically create new tasks in **Trello** whenever you get a new email in Gmail with the label "To-Do." This is an easy way to stay organized and ensure you don't miss important tasks.

3. **Integrating with AI Tools:**
The real power of Zapier lies in its ability to connect AI-powered tools to your workflow. For example, you can use AI tools like **ChatGPT** to automatically generate email replies, content summaries, or even social media posts based on incoming data.

   o **Example:** Set up a Zap where every time a new customer inquiry comes into your email, Zapier sends the message to **ChatGPT** to draft a personalized reply, which is then automatically sent back to the customer.

AI-Powered Automation: From Emails to Social Posts

1. **Automating Emails with AI:**
One of the most common tasks businesses need to automate is email communication. Whether it's follow-up emails, customer inquiries, or marketing campaigns, using AI alongside Zapier can make email management more efficient.

o **Example**: With AI tools like **ChatGPT**, you can automatically generate personalized email responses based on customer inquiries. Combine this with Zapier to send the email without needing to manually write each reply.

o **Process**: Set up a Zap to trigger whenever a new email is received with a specific subject line (e.g., "Customer Support"). This email would then be passed to an AI model, which would generate a relevant response, and Zapier would automatically send it back to the customer.

2. **Social Media Automation with AI**: Social media management is time-consuming, but with AI and Zapier, you can automate much of the process. From posting new content to responding to comments or generating new post ideas, AI can be your virtual social media assistant.

o **Example**: Use **ChatGPT** to generate engaging social media posts based on a prompt like, "Write a post for Instagram about the benefits of mindfulness." Then, connect this with Zapier to automatically schedule the post on platforms like Facebook, Instagram, or LinkedIn at the optimal time for your audience.

3. **Generating Blog or Content Ideas**: Content creation can be a time-consuming process, but with AI-powered tools, you can automate idea generation and outline creation. By integrating these tools with Zapier, you can save valuable time and streamline your content strategy.

o **Example**: Set up a Zap to trigger every Monday morning to automatically generate blog post ideas for the week. Zapier can send a prompt to **ChatGPT**, and based on the generated ideas, it can create drafts that are automatically saved into Google Docs or your preferred project management tool.

4. **Data Management Automation**:
Managing and organizing data from multiple platforms can be a hassle, but Zapier can help automate the process. For example, if you're collecting survey responses or customer feedback, Zapier can automatically organize the data into a Google Sheet, saving you time on manual data entry.

   o **Example**: Use a tool like **Typeform** or **Google Forms** to collect responses, and set up a Zap that automatically inputs the data into a CRM system or project management tool like **Airtable**.

5. **Automating E-commerce Workflows**:
For e-commerce businesses, AI and Zapier can automate everything from inventory management to customer feedback and order confirmations.

   o **Example**: When a customer places an order on your e-commerce platform (e.g., Shopify), a Zap can trigger an email to the customer with tracking information, send the order details to your fulfillment center, and even generate a personalized thank-you message using **ChatGPT**. You can also automate inventory tracking to ensure your stock levels are updated in real-time.

Key Benefits of Combining Zapier and AI for Automation

1. **Time Savings**:
Automating repetitive tasks frees up your time to focus on higher-level activities. By combining AI tools with Zapier, you can automate a wide range of tasks, from generating content to managing emails, social media, and data entry.

2. **Increased Accuracy**:
Human error is a common problem when doing

repetitive tasks manually. By automating workflows, you ensure greater accuracy and consistency, as AI can execute tasks in a precise and error-free manner.

3. **Scalability**:
   As your business grows, automation with Zapier and AI allows you to scale your operations without the need for additional resources. You can easily expand your workflows to handle more tasks and larger volumes of data.

4. **Cost**   **Efficiency**:
   Automating tasks with no-code tools like Zapier and AI reduces the need to hire extra staff or invest in expensive software solutions, making automation accessible and cost-effective for small and medium-sized businesses.

In this chapter, we've seen how **Zapier** and **AI** can work together to create seamless, automated workflows that save you time and increase your productivity. Whether you're automating emails, social media posts, or content generation, combining these tools can help you work smarter, not harder. In the next chapter, we'll dive into how you can further optimize your business by integrating these automated workflows into larger systems for greater efficiency and impact.

Canva + AI: Design Without a Designer

In this chapter, we'll uncover how **Canva**, when combined with AI, allows anyone—entrepreneurs, educators, marketers—to become a visual storyteller without needing a design background. Canva's intuitive drag-and-drop platform now includes powerful AI tools like **Magic Write**, **Text to Image**, and **Brand Kits**, empowering you to create stunning, on-brand designs quickly and efficiently.

Smart Design with Magic Write and AI Tools

1. **What is Magic Write?**
   Magic Write is Canva's built-in AI writing assistant available in Canva Docs. It's designed to help you generate copy for everything from presentations to Instagram captions, blog ideas, and product descriptions.

   o **Example**: Type a prompt like "Write a catchy Instagram caption for a summer clothing sale" and Magic Write will instantly generate creative copy that fits the vibe.

   o **Use case**: Marketers can draft ad copy, social media posts, or product blurbs directly inside Canva, cutting down on time switching between writing and designing tools.

2. **Text to Image Tool**: Canva's AI image generation tool allows you to create custom visuals by describing what you want to see.

   o **Example**: Type "a futuristic classroom with robots teaching children" into the Text to Image tool and instantly get unique illustrations for your content.

   o **Use case**: Educators can bring lessons to life or entrepreneurs can create original visual assets without needing a stock photo subscription.

3. **AI-Powered Layout Suggestions**: Canva suggests layouts, font pairings, and color palettes using AI based on the type of content you're creating—whether it's a pitch deck, Instagram story, or ebook cover.
   o **Use case**: Non-designers can get a head start with professionally designed templates and refine them with their own brand elements.

Branding for Entrepreneurs & Educators

1. **Brand Kits Made Simple**: Canva allows you to set up a **Brand Kit** that includes your brand colors, logos, and fonts. Once it's set, AI helps maintain consistency across all your content.

   o **Use case**: Entrepreneurs can apply their brand look across presentations, social media, business cards, and flyers without needing a designer.

   o **Tip**: Upload your brand assets once and apply them to any design with a single click.

2. **Consistent   Content   Across   Platforms**:
With Canva's AI-enhanced features, you can easily
adapt one piece of content into multiple formats—
Instagram post, Facebook ad, email header, or blog
banner.

   - o **Example**: Create a poster for an event, then
     instantly resize and reformat it for different
     platforms using **Magic Resize**.

   - o **Use case**: Educators and content creators
     can maintain a unified visual presence across
     newsletters, digital classrooms, and social
     media channels.

3. **Templates   for   Every   Purpose**:
Canva has thousands of templates tailored to
entrepreneurs and educators—from course
certificates to email newsletters to pitch decks.
Combined with AI tools like Magic Write and Auto
Enhance (for images), these templates become even
more powerful.

   - o **Use case**: Launching a new course or
     product? Canva lets you whip up a branded
     slide deck, social launch post, and email
     sequence—all in one place.

Why Canva + AI is a Game-Changer

- **Zero Learning Curve**: AI removes guesswork and
  speeds up creation.
- **All-in-One Toolkit**: Combine writing, designing, and
  branding tools in one platform.
- **Saves Time & Money**: No need to hire freelancers or
  purchase separate software.

Pro Tip: Explore Canva's **AI Apps Integration Hub** to
discover even more tools—like AI text summarizers,

background removers, and image enhancers—that can amplify your design workflow.

Part III:

Real-World Applications

AI for Entrepreneurs

Market Research, MVP Validation, and Copywriting Using AI

1. Market Research with AI

AI tools can dramatically simplify and speed up the process of gathering, analyzing, and interpreting market data. You no longer need a research team to understand your audience or industry trends.

How AI Helps:

- **Competitor Analysis**: Tools like **ChatGPT** or **Claude** can scan the web and summarize your competitors' offerings, pricing, and positioning.
- **Trend Discovery**: Use tools like **Exploding Topics**, **Google Trends**, or **ChatGPT plugins** to spot emerging trends.
- **Customer Persona Creation**: AI can help synthesize data into clear, usable customer personas by analyzing behavior patterns from reviews, surveys, and forums.

Example Workflow:

1. Ask ChatGPT:
"Who are the top 5 competitors for a fitness app targeting busy moms?"

2. Follow-up prompt:
"Summarize their strengths, weaknesses, and key differentiators."

3. Use this insight to position your brand or find gaps in the market.

Bonus Tools:

- **Browse AI** (to scrape sites)
- **Glasp or Feedly** (for market content curation)
- **Notion AI** (to summarize long research papers)

2. MVP Validation Using AI

An MVP (Minimum Viable Product) is a simplified version of your product to test its core idea. AI can help you validate your idea faster by simulating users, analyzing feedback, and refining features.

AI Use Cases:

- **Idea** **Validation**:
Ask ChatGPT or Claude:
"What are the risks and advantages of launching a subscription-based journaling app for teens?"

- **Audience** **Poll** **Creation**:
Use **ChatGPT** or **Typeform + Zapier** to draft customer surveys and distribute them.

- **Feedback** **Summary**:
Feed customer responses or reviews into AI tools to get instant sentiment analysis or key pain point summaries

- **Prototype** **Testing**:
Use tools like **Figma AI plugins** or **Tally + Notion AI** to mock up prototypes and test messaging/UX.

Pro Tip:

Pair AI with platforms like **LandingFolio** or **Carrd** to build and test MVP landing pages—then use ChatGPT to write the messaging and analyze signups or conversion feedback.

3. Copywriting Using AI

This is where AI truly shines. Whether it's product descriptions, ad copy, social media posts, or email campaigns, AI can generate, test, and refine persuasive copy in seconds.

Common Copywriting Use Cases:

- **Landing   Pages**:
  Ask ChatGPT:
"Write a headline and subheading for a mobile app that helps users meditate in under 3 minutes."

- **Email   Sequences**:
  Generate multi-step welcome, onboarding, or cart abandonment email flows with tools like **ChatGPT**, **Copy.ai**, or **Jasper**.

- **Ad   Copy**:
  Tailor Facebook/Instagram ads for different audience segments using AI to tweak tone, call to action, and visuals.

- **SEO   Blog   Content**:
  Use ChatGPT + **SurferSEO** to write long-form, keyword-rich content that ranks.

Prompting Tips:

- Be specific with tone and audience:
"Write a friendly and fun Instagram caption for a sustainable clothing brand targeting Gen Z."
- Request multiple versions:
"Give me 3 headline variations for a webinar on AI tools for entrepreneurs."

Best AI Copywriting Tools:

- **ChatGPT** (for versatility)
- **Jasper** (for high-quality marketing copy)
- **Writesonic** (for SEO and blogs)
- **Copy.ai** (for startups and ecommerce)

Bringing It All Together: A Practical Example

Let's say you want to launch a **course on AI tools for digital marketers**.

1. **Market** **Research**:
   Ask ChatGPT to analyze the top AI marketing courses, their content gaps, and pricing.

2. **MVP** **Validation**:
   Build a landing page in **Carrd**, generate email capture copy with **Jasper**, and run a pre-launch waitlist.

3. **Copywriting**:
   Create email campaigns, course descriptions, and social media posts with ChatGPT or Copy.ai—all aligned with your brand voice.

Final Thought

AI doesn't just **save time**—it makes you **smarter, faster, and more strategic**. You no longer need big budgets or a marketing team to perform research, validate an idea, or write great content.
With just **you + AI**, you can move from idea to execution at lightning speed.

Building a Brand with AI Support

Branding is no longer just about logos and color palettes. In today's world, it's about **telling a story**, staying **consistent**, and **connecting emotionally** with your audience. AI tools now empower **non-designers and non-marketers** to build strong, professional brands with speed and confidence.

1. Brand Identity Creation with AI

Before launching a brand, you need to define **who you are**, **what you offer**, and **why it matters**. AI can assist in everything from brand naming to crafting your mission statement.

Tools & Techniques:
- **Name Generators**:
  - Use **ChatGPT** or **Namelix** to generate catchy, SEO-friendly brand names.
  - Prompt: *"Suggest 10 brand name ideas for a women-led eco-friendly skincare startup. Add meanings and domains."*
- **Vision, Mission & Taglines**:
  - ChatGPT can write powerful, emotional mission and vision statements based on your goals and values.
  - Prompt: *"Write a vision and mission statement for a mental health coaching brand focused on teens."*
- **Audience Personas**:
  - AI can analyze demographics and create ideal customer personas for you.
  - Prompt: *"Create 3 user personas for a subscription-based productivity app targeting remote freelancers."*

2. Visual Branding with AI

Your brand's look and feel matters. AI-powered design tools now help you create logos, color schemes, typography, and layouts with little to no design skills.

Tools:
- **Canva** (with AI tools like Magic Design & Brand Kits)

**You Can Do AI: How Non-Coders Can Create, Design &
Automate with AI Tools**

- **Looka**, **LogoAI**, or **Designs.ai** (for logo generation)
- **Khroma** or **Coolors** (for AI-generated color palettes)

Use AI To:

- **Generate a Logo**:
  - o Use tools like Looka or Canva's logo creator.
    Provide your brand name, industry, and style
    preference, and the AI gives you multiple
    options.
- **Choose a Color Palette**:
  - o AI tools suggest harmonious color palettes
    based on your brand values (e.g., calm,
    energetic, elegant).
- **Set Fonts & Typography**:
  - o Let AI suggest font combinations based on
    your tone—modern, classic, fun, or
    professional.
- **Create a Brand Kit**:
  - o Canva's Brand Hub helps you set your
    brand's fonts, colors, logo, and voice in one
    place for instant, consistent application.

3. Voice, Tone & Messaging with AI

AI can help define how your brand "sounds"—your tone of
voice, vocabulary, and emotional appeal across platforms.

Key Messaging AI Can Help With:

- **Elevator Pitch**:
  - o Prompt: *"Create a 2-line elevator pitch for a
    budget travel app for college students."*
- **Taglines & Slogans**:
  - o Prompt: *"Generate 5 catchy, friendly taglines
    for a plant-based snack brand."*
- **Social Media Bio**:
  - o Prompt: *"Write a fun yet professional
    Instagram bio for a digital wellness coach."*
- **Brand Voice Guidelines**:
  - o Prompt: *"Based on this content, describe the
    brand voice in 3 adjectives and give voice
    do's and don'ts."*

4. Content & Storytelling with AI

AI enables you to create on-brand content at scale—blog posts, emails, website copy, and social content that aligns with your voice and goals.

Tools:
- **ChatGPT / Jasper** – For website copy, ad content, storytelling
- **Copy.ai** – For sales funnels, email sequences, value propositions
- **Canva Magic Write** – For social captions, headlines, and longer-form content inside Canva docs

AI in Action:
- Write your **About Us** page with:

"Write an 'About Us' section for a sustainable clothing brand that values minimalism and female empowerment."

- Generate **social post ideas** with:

"Give me 10 Instagram post ideas for a small vegan bakery launching a new cookie flavor."
- Draft **ad copy** for Google, Facebook, or Instagram.

5. Brand Consistency Across Platforms

AI helps ensure your brand appears polished and consistent everywhere, from emails to videos to presentations.

Automation Tips:

- Use **Zapier + ChatGPT**: Automatically draft branded email responses, blog summaries, or social posts.
- **Canva Templates**: Use branded templates for everything—proposals, posts, reels, pitch decks.
- **Notion AI**: Maintain a living brand manual with your colors, tone, bios, and sample messaging.

6. Monitor, Refine & Grow Your Brand

After launching, you can use AI to monitor your brand's performance and adjust accordingly.

Tools:

- **Brand24 or Hootsuite AI** – To track mentions, sentiment, and brand perception.
- **Google Alerts + ChatGPT** – Summarize and analyze brand mentions or reviews.
- **Surveys with AI Analysis** – Collect customer feedback via Typeform, then use AI to summarize insights and adjust your messaging or product.

Final Thoughts

AI doesn't replace creativity—it enhances it. With the right tools and prompts, you can build a **polished, professional, personality-packed brand** without needing a full team.

Whether you're a **first-time founder**, **freelancer**, or **educator**, AI is your silent cofounder—helping you build a brand that connects, converts, and grows.

AI for Marketers

1. Content Generation Using AI Tools

What It Is:

Content generation is the process of creating written, visual, or audio content for marketing, blogs, emails, websites, etc. AI tools help automate and streamline this process.

How It Works:

AI models (like GPT-4) are trained on vast datasets, learning how humans write and communicate. These tools can generate:
- Blog posts
- Ad copy
- Social captions
- Product descriptions
- Scripts
- Newsletters

Key Features:

- **Prompt-based Writing**: You enter a topic or a few keywords, and the tool writes content.
- **Templates**: Pre-built formats for emails, product listings, blog intros, etc.
- **Tone and Style Settings**: Adjust the tone (formal, casual, witty, etc.) to match your brand.
- **Multilingual Support**: Some tools generate content in multiple languages.

Popular Tools:

- **ChatGPT / Jasper** – for blog posts, copywriting, emails.
- **Copy.ai / Writesonic** – for quick marketing copy.
- **Surfer AI / Scalenut** – blog articles optimized for SEO.
- **Canva / Lumen5** – for visual + text content creation (infographics, videos).

2. SEO Optimization Using AI Tools

What It Is:

SEO (Search Engine Optimization) is about improving your content so it ranks higher in search engine results. AI tools now automate much of the keyword research, on-page optimization, and content gap analysis.

How It Works:

AI tools crawl the top-ranking pages for a keyword and reverse-engineer what's working. Then they help you:
- Find relevant keywords and clusters
- Structure articles (headers, word count, etc.)
- Optimize meta tags and internal links
- Identify content gaps and opportunities

Key Features:

- **Keyword Suggestion**: Based on trends, difficulty, and search volume.
- **Competitor Analysis**: See what your rivals are ranking for.
- **Content Score**: AI grades your draft against top-performing pages.
- **SERP Analysis**: Real-time insights from Google's results page.

Popular Tools:

- **Surfer SEO** – integrates with content editors to guide writing.
- **Clearscope / MarketMuse** – optimize existing or new content with semantic keywords.
- **Ahrefs / SEMrush** – track keywords, backlinks, and SEO performance.
- **Frase** – content brief creation + optimization suggestions.

3. Social Media Scheduling Using AI Tools

What It Is:

This is the practice of planning, creating, and automating social media posts in advance. AI tools help with writing posts, choosing optimal times, and analyzing performance.

How It Works:

You input the content or let AI generate it. Then, you schedule it across platforms (Instagram, Twitter/X, LinkedIn, etc.) with suggested times for engagement. AI also learns from past performance to improve recommendations.

Key Features:

- **Auto-Generated Captions**: AI writes engaging posts from blogs or headlines.
- **Best Time to Post**: Based on historical data and engagement patterns.
- **Content Calendar**: Visual dashboard to plan weeks or months ahead.
- **Cross-Platform Publishing**: Post to multiple platforms in one go.
- **Analytics**: Track clicks, likes, comments, and adjust strategy.

Popular Tools:

- **Buffer / Hootsuite / Later** – standard scheduling + analytics.
- **Lately.ai** – turns long content (like blogs, podcasts) into dozens of social posts.
- **Missinglettr** – builds entire social campaigns from a blog post.
- **CoSchedule** – content calendar + AI headline analyzer.

Summary Table:

Function	Purpose	Best AI Tools
Content Generation	Write blogs, ads, emails, captions	ChatGPT, Jasper, Copy.ai, Canva
SEO Optimization	Rank higher in Google	Surfer SEO, Clearscope, SEMrush
Social Scheduling	Automate and optimize social media posts	Buffer, Lately.ai, Missinglettr

AI for Content Creators

AI is a serious game-changer for content creators—streamlining the creative process, saving hours, and boosting engagement. Whether you're a YouTuber, Instagram creator, podcaster, or brand, AI tools can help with:

1. Scripts, Captions, and Video Ideas

Script Writing

AI can generate full scripts for:

- YouTube videos
- Reels/TikToks
- Podcast intros/outros
- Webinars or how-to tutorials

How It Works:

- Input a topic or idea.
- AI structures it with hooks, storytelling, and call-to-actions.
- You can choose tone (funny, serious, informative) and format (narrative, listicle, interview, etc.).

Tools:

- **ChatGPT / Jasper** – custom scripts for any format.
- **Synthesia** – turns text into AI video scripts with avatars.
- **Descript** – auto-generates podcast and video transcripts + script writing.

Captions & Subtitles

AI writes compelling captions or extracts key phrases from video/audio.

Features:

- Captions optimized for engagement (questions, emojis, hashtags).
- Auto-subtitling for accessibility and reach.
- SEO-friendly YouTube descriptions and tags.

Tools:

- **Copy.ai / CaptionAI** – short-form captions for Instagram, TikTok.
- **Pictory / VEED.io** – auto-generate subtitles + style them.
- **YouTube Studio AI** – helps write titles, tags, and video descriptions.

Video Ideas & Trends

AI tools suggest fresh content angles based on:

- Current trends
- What's working for competitors
- Audience behavior

Tools:

- **VidIQ / TubeBuddy** – video idea generators + trend tracking on YouTube.
- **ChatGPT** – brainstorm video themes, hooks, and angles.
- **TikTok Creative Center AI** – find trending formats and music.

2. Repurposing Content with AI

Why create from scratch every time? AI lets you **turn one piece of content into 10+ others,** keeping your brand message consistent across platforms.

Repurpose Long-Form into Short-Form

AI can take a blog post, podcast, or webinar and break it into:

- Instagram carousels
- YouTube Shorts / Reels
- Twitter threads
- LinkedIn posts
- Email snippets

Example: Take a 10-minute video → get:

- 3 TikTok clips
- 5 social captions
- A blog summary
- An email newsletter

Tools:

- **Lately.ai** – turns long-form content into dozens of social posts.
- **Pictory** – cuts videos into highlight clips automatically.
- **Descript** – edits audio/video and creates bite-sized clips with captions.
- **ContentFries** – repurposes one video into multiple posts for different platforms.

Transcripts & Blog Conversions

- AI transcribes your video or podcast and turns it into a blog post or article.
- Great for SEO and reaching non-video audiences.

Tools:

- **Otter.ai / Descript** – transcription + text cleanup.
- **QuillBot** – rewrite transcripts into polished blog posts.
- **Surfer SEO** – optimize repurposed blogs for search.

Summary of Benefits

Use Case	AI Advantage	Tools to Use
Video Script Writing	Saves time, better structure	ChatGPT, Jasper, Descript
Caption Generation	Faster posting, higher engagement	CaptionAI, Copy.ai, Pictory
Content Ideas	Stay on trend, never run out of ideas	VidIQ, TubeBuddy, ChatGPT
Repurposing Content	Maximize content mileage across platforms	Lately.ai, ContentFries, Descript
Blog from Podcast/Video	Boosts SEO, reaches more audiences	Otter.ai, Surfer SEO, QuillBot

AI for Educators

AI tools help teachers work smarter—not harder. They streamline planning, automate assessments, and support individualized instruction, making education more efficient, engaging, and inclusive.

1. Creating Lesson Plans and Quizzes

Lesson Plan Generation

AI can help design full lesson plans in minutes, including:

- Learning objectives
- Class activities
- Discussion prompts
- Homework assignments
- Timing and pacing

How It Works:

- Enter the topic, grade level, and curriculum goals.
- AI aligns plans with educational standards (e.g., Common Core, NGSS).
- You can customize by class size, teaching style, or available time.

Tools:

- **ChatGPT** – builds custom lesson plans with structure and creativity.
- **Curipod** – interactive slide-based lessons with AI support.
- **Eduaide.AI** – designed specifically for teachers to create activities, plans, and rubrics.

Quiz and Test Creation

AI can auto-generate:

- Multiple choice questions (MCQs)
- Short answer or essay questions
- True/false or matching sets
- Auto-graded quizzes

Features:

- Difficulty adjustment (basic to advanced)
- Automatic answer keys
- AI feedback on student responses
- Integration into Google Classroom, LMS platforms

Tools:

- **Quizizz / Kahoot! AI** – fun, gamified quizzes created in minutes.
- **Teachermatic** – instantly builds quizzes aligned to topics or textbooks.
- **QuestionWell** – AI-powered quiz bank generator for teachers.

2. Personalized Learning at Scale

Tailoring Instruction to Each Student

You Can Do AI: How Non-Coders Can Create, Design & Automate with AI Tools

AI allows teachers to meet diverse learning needs without hours of prep work. It helps by:

- Diagnosing skill gaps
- Recommending targeted practice
- Adapting difficulty in real-time

How It Works:

- AI analyzes student responses, engagement, and performance.
- It adjusts lessons or materials to fit individual progress and style.
- Teachers get insights to group students or offer 1-on-1 support.

Examples:

- A struggling reader gets extra phonics exercises.
- A fast learner gets advanced problem-solving challenges.
- ESL students get simplified content with vocabulary support.

Tools:

- **Khanmigo (by Khan Academy)** – AI tutor + teacher assistant.
- **Socratic by Google** – helps students learn through guided questions.
- **Century Tech / Knewton** – adaptive learning platforms for math, science, and reading.

Feedback and Assessment Automation

AI tools provide instant, personalized feedback on:

- Essays
- Math problems
- Programming code
- Language use

This reduces grading time and gives students quicker insight.

Tools:

- **Gradescope AI** – streamlines grading and provides consistent feedback.
- **NoRedInk** – personalized grammar and writing practice with adaptive difficulty.
- **Formative** – gives real-time data on student comprehension during lessons.

Summary: How AI Empowers Educators

Task	AI Solution	Tools to Use
Lesson Plan Creation	Auto-structured plans aligned with standards	Eduaide, ChatGPT, Curipod
Quiz & Test Generation	Instant, customizable assessments	Quizizz, Teachermatic, QuestionWell
Personalized Learning	Adaptive content, AI tutors	Khanmigo, Century Tech, NoRedInk
Automated Feedback	Instant grading, deeper insights	Gradescope, Formative

Part IV:

Responsible Use & Next Steps

Husn Ara
Ethics, Bias, and Limitations of AI

AI is powerful, but it's not perfect. Using it responsibly means understanding its **ethical implications**, recognizing **bias**, and setting clear **boundaries** on what it should and shouldn't do.

1. How to Use AI Responsibly

Be Transparent

When using AI in your work—whether in writing, teaching, or content creation—**disclose it** when it matters. If you're using AI to generate a report, assist with lesson plans, or write copy, be open about it to build trust.

Maintain Human Oversight

AI should **assist**, not **replace** critical thinking. Always:

- Review AI-generated content for accuracy and relevance.
- Fact-check data and references.
- Add your personal or professional judgment.

Respect Privacy and Data Ethics

AI tools often rely on user input and data to operate. Avoid feeding them:

- Private student info
- Confidential business plans
- Sensitive customer data

Use tools that follow data protection laws (GDPR, FERPA, HIPAA, etc.).

Follow Platform and Legal Guidelines

Different industries and platforms (like education, publishing, or advertising) have rules about how AI can be used. Make sure:

- You're not violating terms of service (e.g., by automating test answers).
- You're complying with copyright and licensing standards.

2. Avoiding Over-Reliance and Plagiarism

Don't Let AI Think for You

AI can sound confident—even when it's wrong. Over-reliance can lead to:

- Surface-level ideas with no depth.
- Mistakes going unnoticed.
- Lack of originality in creative work.

What to Do:

- Use AI for drafts, structure, or brainstorming—not final output.
- Always personalize, refine, and fact-check.

Watch for AI-Generated Plagiarism

AI generates content by mimicking patterns from its training data. This can lead to:

- Unintentional reuse of common phrases.
- Similar wording to existing content.
- Inadvertent copyright issues.

Best Practices:

- Use plagiarism checkers (like Turnitin, Grammarly, Copyscape).
- Rewrite and inject your own voice into the AI output.
- Never publish raw AI content without editing.

Be Critical of AI Bias

AI is trained on human-created data, which means it can **reflect and amplify existing biases**, such as:

- Gender or racial stereotypes
- Cultural insensitivity
- Biased assumptions in educational or hiring tools

How to Handle It:

- Test AI outputs for fairness and inclusivity.
- Diversify prompts to detect and reduce bias.
- Don't assume AI is neutral—it's not.

Summary: Responsible AI Use Checklist

Concern	What to Watch For	What to Do
Transparency	Are you hiding your use of AI?	Be upfront when AI helps with work
Accuracy	Does AI ever hallucinate or mislead?	Always double-check facts
Bias	Are outputs reinforcing stereotypes?	Test for fairness and review language
Plagiarism	Could AI reuse content too closely?	Use plagiarism tools and rewrite in your voice
Privacy	Are you sharing private or sensitive data?	Keep identifiable info out of AI inputs
Over-Reliance	Is AI doing *too much* thinking for you?	Add your judgment, context, and creativity

What's Next? The Future of No-Code AI

AI is no longer just for data scientists. With **no-code AI**, people with **zero programming experience** can build smart apps, automate workflows, generate content, and analyze data—using drag-and-drop tools, natural language, or simple forms.
And it's only getting easier.

1. Emerging Tools and Trends

Here's what's shaping the future of no-code AI right now:

AI Workflows & Automation Platforms

New platforms are merging AI with automation tools to let you:

- Build chatbots
- Trigger actions based on AI responses
- Automate entire business workflows

Trending Tools:

- **Zapier AI** – create automations using natural language ("When I get an email, summarize it and send to Slack").

- **Make (Integromat)** – drag-and-drop AI-enhanced workflows.
- **Notion AI / Airtable AI** – smart databases that analyze and act on your data.

AI App Builders

You can now build AI-powered tools and apps without touching code:

- Personal AI assistants
- AI-powered forms, search, chat interfaces

Trending Tools:

- **Glide** – build mobile apps with AI-enhanced logic.
- **Bubble + OpenAI plugin** – create custom AI apps visually.
- **Adalo** – no-code app development with AI support.

Text-to-Everything Interfaces

We're moving from prompts to platforms. No-code AI tools now let you:

- Type what you want ("make me a landing page") and get it done.
- Control entire websites, videos, and data flows using plain English.

Examples:

- **Durable AI** – builds websites from a single sentence.
- **Runway** – generates videos from text input.
- **Promptly / Replit AI** – build apps using AI as your coding co-pilot.

Multimodal AI Integration

No-code tools are beginning to combine **text, image, video, and data** inputs/outputs.

Examples:

- **Pika / Synthesia** – generate video from script + voice + design style.

- **Uizard** – turn hand-drawn UI sketches into functional prototypes.

2. Staying Ahead Without Learning to Code

You don't need to be a developer to use AI like one. Here's how to stay current and competitive:

Learn the Tools, Not the Code

- Focus on how tools *work*, not how they're built.
- Choose 2–3 AI platforms in your field (marketing, education, content creation) and master them.

Use AI to Build, Test, and Scale Ideas

- Validate business ideas or product prototypes without hiring devs.
- Build MVPs (minimum viable products) using tools like Glide, Bubble, or ChatGPT + Zapier.

Understand AI Capabilities and Limitations

- Stay aware of what AI can and *can't* do (bias, privacy, hallucination).
- Follow AI ethics and use policies, especially in regulated fields.

Follow Key Voices and Trends

- Substack newsletters, Twitter/X threads, LinkedIn creators are constantly sharing new use cases.
- Track product launches from OpenAI, Google, Microsoft, and leading startups.

Summary: The Future of No-Code AI

Trend	What It Means for You	Tools to Try
AI-Driven Automations	Automate work without coding	Zapier AI, Make, Notion AI
Drag-and-Drop AI App Builders	Build custom tools visually	Glide, Bubble, Adalo
Text-to-Website & Text-to-App	Describe what you want, AI builds it	Durable, Promptly, Uizard
Video & Design Generation	AI handles creative content production	Runway, Synthesia, Pika
Cross-Platform Smart Workflows	Mix text, video, images, databases easily	Airtable AI, Replit AI, Canva Magic Studio

Final Thought:

You don't need to learn how to code. You just need to learn how to **communicate with AI tools**— clearly, creatively, and responsibly.

Toolbox & Resources

Whether you're a creator, educator, marketer, or entrepreneur, having the right tools and support system can turn AI from "cool tech" into **daily leverage**. Here's what you need to get going or level up.

1. Recommended Tools & Templates

You Can Do AI: How Non-Coders Can Create, Design & Automate with AI Tools

These tools help you **create, automate, teach, or build**—without needing to code.

Content Creation & Marketing

Task	Tools
Blog & Copywriting	ChatGPT, Jasper, Copy.ai
SEO Optimization	Surfer SEO, Clearscope, Frase
Social Captions	Lately.ai, Buffer AI Assistant, Canva
Email Campaigns	Mailchimp AI, ConvertKit, BeeFree

Education & Lesson Planning

Task	Tools
Lesson Plans & Quizzes	Eduaide.AI, Curipod, Quizizz, Teachermatic
Adaptive Learning	Khanmigo, NoRedInk, Century Tech
Transcription/Feedback	Descript, Gradescope, Otter.ai

No-Code Building & Automation

Task	Tools
App/Website Building	Glide, Bubble, Durable, Softr
Automation & Workflows	Zapier AI, Make, TallyForms
AI Image/Video Creation	Canva Magic Studio, Runway, Pika

Repurposing & Scripting

Task	Tools
Repurpose Content	Lately.ai, ContentFries, Pictory
Script/Voice Gen	Descript, Synthesia, ElevenLabs

AI Templates to Start Fast

Here are **plug-and-play templates** to help you get moving quickly:

Template Type	Where to Find
AI Content Prompts	AIPRM for ChatGPT, PromptHero
Social Media Post Ideas	Canva Templates, Jasper AI Recipes
Lesson Plans & Rubrics	Eduaide.AI, Curipod Library
Email & Landing Pages	BeeFree Templates, Mailchimp AI
Workflow Blueprints	Zapier Playbooks, Glide Templates

2. Communities, Courses & Further Learning

Communities (Ask, Share, Get Inspired)

Platform	Description
r/NoCode (Reddit)	For building apps & automation without code
Maven.com	Live cohort-based courses on AI & tools
Indie Hackers	For solopreneurs building with AI
AI Tool Report Discord	Discuss new AI tools and prompt ideas
Teachers Using AI (FB Group)	Practical tips for educators

Courses & Tutorials

Platform	Focus Area
FutureTools.io	Weekly updates + curated tool list
Buildspace	Learn to build with AI tools
Coursera / edX	AI for non-coders, intro to GPT
YouTube Channels	Free, tool-specific walkthroughs
Learn Prompting	Hands-on guide to writing better AI prompts

News & Updates

Source	What You Get
Ben's Bites (Newsletter)	Daily AI news, tools, use cases
The Rundown AI	Short summaries of what's new
Medium AI Blogs	Real-world applications

Final Tip:

Build your **own custom AI stack**:

- Pick 2 tools you use daily (ex: ChatGPT + Canva)
- Pick 1 tool for automation (ex: Zapier or Notion AI)
- Pick 1 learning hub or community

Start small, iterate, and plug in more tools as your needs grow.

AI Dashboard Structure in Notion

Here's a simple, powerful layout you can customize. I'll break it into sections you can copy-paste into your own Notion, with ideas for what to include in each.

Dashboard Title:

My AI Toolkit & Learning Hub

1. Quick Access: Favorite Tools

A gallery or list view of tools you use daily.

Tool	Use Case	Link
ChatGPT	Writing, planning	chat.openai.com
Canva	Design, visuals	canva.com
Zapier AI	Automations	zapier.com
Jasper AI	Marketing copy	jasper.ai

2. Templates & Prompts Library

Use toggles, subpages, or a database to store your favorite prompts and templates.

Example Categories:

- ◆ Blog Post Prompt
- ◆ Lesson Plan Generator
- ◆ Social Media Caption Formula
- ◆ Video Script Starter

[Blog Prompt Template]
> "Write a 600-word blog post on [topic] targeting [audience], with a [tone] tone. Include a headline, intro, 3 subheads, and a call-to-action."

[Lesson Plan Prompt]

> "Create a 45-minute lesson plan for grade [X] about [topic],
including objectives, activities, materials, and exit ticket."

3. Weekly Learning Tracker

Table or board view for tracking what you're learning or
testing.

Week	Topic/Tool	Resource	Status
1	Notion AI basics	YouTube – Thomas Frank	✅ Done
2	Prompt Engineering	LearnPrompting.org	🔄 In Progress
3	Zapier workflows	Zapier Playbooks	⏳ To Start

4. Tool Categories (Linked Databases or Pages)

Create pages for each category with embedded links, tips, or
resources.

Examples:

- **Content Creation**
  - ChatGPT, Jasper, Copy.ai
- **Education & Lesson Planning**
  - Eduaide, Curipod, Quizizz
- **Automation Tools**
  - Zapier AI, Make, TallyForms
- **Video & Design**
  - Canva Magic, Runway, Pictory

Each subpage can include:

- What it's for
- Best use cases
- Links & tutorials
- Template examples

5. Community & Course Links

Quick-access buttons or links to stay plugged in:

- r/NoCode (Reddit)
- Buildspace
- FutureTools.io
- Ben's Bites Newsletter
- The Rundown AI

Bonus: Idea Dump / Future Projects

Use a simple table or kanban board to collect:

- Content ideas
- AI app ideas
- Automations to try
- New tools to test